How to Conduct a Successful Board Meeting

Pastor Jeff Culver

Copyright © 2018 Jeff Culver

All rights reserved.

ISBN: 9781718150652
Independently published

All Scripture is from the World English Bible, The World English Bible (WEB) is a Public Domain (no copyright) Modern English translation of the Holy Bible.

DEDICATION:

To my wife, who inspired me to write.

CONTENTS

	Blessing	i
1	INTRODUCTION OF AUTHOR	1
2	THE MANY FACES OF A CHURCH BOARD	6
3	LEARN THE CHURCH'S LEADERSHIP HISTORY	11
4	PARLIMENTARY PROCEDURE	17
5	WRITING THE AGENDA	27
6	CALLING A BOARD MEETING	38
7	THE BOARD MEETING	42
8	AFTER THE MEETING	52
9	EMERGENCY MEETINGS	56

BLESSING

May God's blessing be upon you as you serve His people in both their joys and their sorrows.

1 INTRODUCTION OF AUTHOR

Organization of Book

Thank you for looking at this short book. My prayer is that it will bless you in your board relations if you've been leading churches for years or if you are just beginning to. I am beginning this book with a personal introduction to illustrate both my background and my experience, which is wide and varied. I then move into some other important preliminary details that heavily influence a church board and the way they think and act. A wise pastor will examine outside influences that seem to not be specific to setting an agenda, getting issues decided and work accomplished. Many things such as culture, history, local customs and congregational power brokers wield much more influence on the process between a pastor and board than might be expected.

After a brief survey of outside influences, I will then move into the process itself.

I have been in the full-time ministry for 22 years, and have served as a Senior Pastor since May of 1998. Ministry has brought my wife, Kathryn, and I to some of the most amazing places in the United States, places that many people vacation at, yet we have had the privilege to live there. Having raised our two boys, Dion and Stefan, we are now learning how to live with an empty nest.

I began my full-time ministry journey at Lake City Assembly of God in Medical Lake, WA, just outside of Spokane as their youth pastor. It was here that I learned the foundation that I would build my ministry style and ideals upon. After serving about two years as a youth pastor, I felt the call of God to venture into the pulpit, not knowing what awaited me.

Angoon Assembly of God in Angoon, AK would be the church that I would be my first senior pastorate, and it was here that I quickly realized that what I had learned in Bible School had not fully prepared me for the major life events, such as wedding and funerals, or the leading of church board meetings that I would now be fully responsible for. Angoon is in one of the most beautiful parts of the world, Southeast Alaska, and the Tlingit people are even more wonderful than the scenery that is found along the famous Inside Passage. Here, I learned how to work with a church board. Here I first learned the many details of leading a church board. It was here that I also officiated my first wedding and performed my first funeral. This church was so gracious with this new pastor and I will be forever grateful to them.

After three and a half years, I had felt a very distinct leading of God to move to another church, and shortly thereafter found myself leading Dillingham Assembly of God in Dillingham, AK. Dillingham is found in Western Alaska on the north end of Bristol Bay, and is traditionally the home of Yupik Eskimo people, though the community itself is now very multi-cultural in its makeup. Three years later, after perhaps the most profound experience with God that I have ever had, I was called to the state of Minnesota.

Moving to Minnesota was quite an adventure for my 2 boys, my wife, the family dog (an energetic border collie and husky mix) and myself. We had to fly our four-wheel drive club cab Chevy pickup truck with my snowmobile in the bed of it from Dillingham to Anchorage on a C-130, where the ultimate horror story began. You have heard of airlines losing luggage, but how do you lose a four-wheel drive truck with a snowmobile in the back? Dillingham insisted they flew it to Anchorage while Anchorage insisted it was still in Dillingham. After a few hours, they thankfully located our truck in Anchorage and we were able to begin the long drive to Detroit Lakes, MN.

Detroit Lakes, MN, located about 45 minutes west of Fargo, ND (which is nothing like it is depicted in the movie, Fargo), and is known as a major part of Minnesota Lakes Country, and a popular vacation destination, is where we would spend the next 11 years of our lives, pastoring the wonderful people of Detroit Lakes Assembly of God. Here, we were immersed in yet another very distinct culture, the Scandinavian culture of the Upper Midwest.

After our children graduated from high school and were in college and beginning their own lives, the Lord moved on us again to relocate to another strange and exotic land where we find ourselves ministering at the time of this writing, on St. Croix in the US Virgin Islands, from Alaska to a tropical paradise. The vast majority of the members of our congregation are not native to St.

Croix, but come from the many different island-nations that make up the Lesser Antilles.

To those who are wondering, yes, we have experienced hurricanes, two which were Category 5 and took a direct hit from Hurricane Maria, which destroyed three of the church's buildings. Perhaps one day I will write a book on how to lead building projects, as I have led many over the years.

Occasion for Writing

As you can see, our ministry has been very unique in that we have lived and ministered in a variety of very different cultures, each of which have a very different set of cultural expectations.

While cultures may vary greatly across the United States and other nations, there are some constants that transcend culture. My prayer is that this guide will assist the new pastor in administrating successful board meetings, and inspire experienced pastors to turn board meetings into positive and productive experiences.

2 THE MANY FACES OF A CHURCH BOARD

As I mentioned in the introduction, I have had the privilege of leading churches in many cultures. The denomination that I minister in is a congregational denomination. This means among other things that the congregation nominates and elects the church board. The church board is made of up an odd number of members. Some churches call these members trustees, others deacons and others elders. For most purposes, despite the difference in title there is little difference in their function.

The church boards that I have worked with have been very different from one another in many ways. I have led boards that were made up of three members to as many as seven. I have led all-male boards and all-female boards, as well as mixed-gender boards. At the time of this writing, the board of the church that I serve consists of four males and one female, and each one is a powerful leader in their own way. I believe that both males and females bring unique perspectives to the board meeting.

Every Church Has its Own Culture

One thing that I have learned in the past twenty years is that the local culture plays a large part in the culture of the church. For this reason, every church has a separate and distinct culture unique to itself. Taking the time to get to know the history of the community you serve, and experiencing its culture is an important investment in successful communication, the importance of which cannot be understated. Church boards are going to communicate in their unique cultural context, using their city or regions unique colloquial expressions.

While in Alaska, fishing expressions went far beyond the business of fishing, filling daily life and communication. Native American culture also played a large role, particularly during my tenure in Angoon. Angoon is an ancient Tlingit village, and is known for keeping alive the traditions of their ancestors. This is particularly expressed through the death ritual, which is very different from the traditional western Protestant way. By participating in their culture, I not only learned how to effectively communicate with them, but also learned a few things to apply to my own life that I will carry with me all my days.

In Minnesota, a dominantly Scandinavian population, culture was extremely different. Minnesota has its own expressions, and they take time to learn. Expressions such as "o-fer" and uff da filled conversations. After a while, I came to realize that uff da fits about anywhere, while o-fer is short for "oh for". Being raised in the Pacific Northwest, if I wanted to say something was cute, I would say "Isn't that cute?" A Minnesotan would say "O-fer cute."

Here in the Caribbean, where I lead a church while writing this, I had to learn a whole different form of communication again. The unique element here (besides the obvious lack of snow or any temperature below 70F) is that the vast majority of the church, over 90%, were born in other nations. My current board consists of people born in St. Lucia, Trinidad, Antigua and Dominica. The Caribbean accent is difficult to acclimate to at first, and take a good amount of effort. Part of this is because of the rapid speech and strong accent. For instance, most do not pronounce the "th" in words, just the "t". Everything then, becomes "everyt'ing". They have different manners of greeting and speaking. The phrase "good night" to this northern man was always used as a concluding remark. In the Caribbean, it is a greeting. It is very important culturally to greet according to the time of day, be it morning, afternoon or night.

When greeting a stranger, it is customary for them to acknowledge your greeting with a simple "all right". Later when they get to know you it becomes more interactive.

You might be wondering why I am writing all this about culture to begin a book on that exciting topic of church board meetings. The reason is that the culture of a community and region differs greatly from place to place. Even though I have served in the same denomination for over twenty years, I have never experienced two churches who are culturally the same. Doctrinally, yes, but culturally, no. Learning to communicate and understand what is being said is vital to leading a church and a church board meeting.

Different Financial Situations

The church's financial standing is also going to play a large part in the interaction of a board meeting. Take the time to get to become familiar with the financial situation of the church, preferably before you accept the pastorate, but if that is not possible, do so as quickly as possible.

I've led churches with little to no funds, and churches that are approaching six figures in their bank account. Financial standing affects the dynamics of the board.

3 LEARN THE CHURCH'S LEADERSHIP HISTORY

There is one final important element to take into consideration that will play a large part, particularly in the first three years of ministry, in the pastor and board relationship. That element is the past history of leadership in the church. Take the time to ask questions regarding the relationship between your predecessor and the board. Discover if there were problems, conflict, or close relations. Learn why the previous minister left. Did they leave on good or bad terms, of their own volition or were they asked to leave?

I have led churches where previous ministries departed on very bad terms, and discovered that the hostility felt during the heat of conflict transfers to the next minister. Sometimes it is intentional, but most of the time unintentionally. It is, however, something that will have to be resolved, and it is important to know that it is going to have an effect on the early relationship.

Take the time to access records of board meetings and agendas from the previous administration, it will give you a good idea of how the board operated in the past and the climate that it operated in. Make a thorough analysis of the history of the church. As I mentioned above, churches are very different from one another, even though they may be of the same denominational affiliation. Don't assume that because you are a Baptist minister, that all Baptist churches are the same, or if you are a Methodist, all Methodist churches are the same. Doctrinally, they will be similar, but each church emphasizes one particular point over another even there. Rest assured, that culturally, there are great differences, even over a short distance.

I have found that one of the very best sources of historical information regarding the church are senior citizens who have been attending the church most of their lives. Most of the time, they are very forthcoming about details, both good and bad, and for the most part enjoy talking about the history of their church. Over the years, they have experienced both the good and the bad, and can give you much needed insight into current and past leadership.

Know the By-Laws

Become very familiar with the by-laws of your church. This is of particular importance in congregational churches. My denomination, the Assemblies of God, is congregational in government. Our district leadership recommends by-laws to the various churches in the region, but each church can amend and adopt with a fair degree of latitude. As such, I've never seen two sets of by-laws the same. The by-laws are the rules you will have to follow, so make sure to read them and follow them as closely as possible.

Most churches also have a self-appointed "lawyer" in a position of power. It is a good idea to ask what their interpretation of the by-laws is, not so that you as pastor can be governed by their interpretation, but so that you can gain an understanding of perception. This person's perception has probably carried a lot of weight in the past, and will greatly influence the expectations and activities of the board.

In one church I led, I had a couple who were the local lawyers, self-appointed, of course. Like most people with an interest in following rules properly, they really are good people, they just had a different view of by-laws. I was told by one of them that the by-laws came from God. They held the by-laws as equal to scripture itself. This was a very important revelation for me and my working with them over the years. Both spouses were elected more than once to the church board over my tenure there.

More than likely, you will be expected to think in line with the local lawyer's interpretation, so it is very helpful to learn the nuances from the source. Searching out their interpretation of the by-laws also gains favor with them, particularly because most leaders will run afoul of these interpretations accidently more than once. It smooths things over simply because you initiated the discussion, and demonstrates that you care for the local priorities.

Examine Previous Records

Finally, examine previous records. If possible, read the minutes from the final year of your predecessor's tenure. This will give you more insight into the actual workings of the board than anything else. These records will let you get to know the board members before you ever meet with them. They will reveal how each one votes, what their priorities are, if they are supportive or prone to disagreements. Taking the time to read a year's worth of records will bring behavioral patterns to light and individual priorities among the board.

Reviewing the previous administration's agendas will reveal how the board meetings are accustomed to being conducted. These will reveal the former minister's priorities and emphasis. It is important to know what people are used to, the familiar sets people at ease, particularly in new situations. Knowing what the previous emphasis was gives you a starting point to transition the church towards your own priorities.

Jeff Culver

4 PARLIAMENTARY PROCEDURE

Most churches, as non-profit organizations, need to conduct regular business meetings. A basic understanding of parliamentary procedure is important when preparing to conduct these meetings. Parliamentary procedure is a set of rules that allows for orderly meetings. Robert's Rules of Order is the authority on parliamentary procedure, and every minister should own a copy. In this chapter, I am going to give a brief overview of parliamentary procedure, with a particular focus on how it impacts writing an agenda and conducting the meeting itself.

Parliamentary procedure establishes a consistent structure for board meeting agendas. This is consistency greatly reduces the stress of writing agendas, and also reduces stress for board members, as they have a sense of familiarity with the meeting structure. Adhering to parliamentary procedure's recommended structure keeps agenda-writing organized and productive. I will discuss this aspect in more detail in following chapters.

Parliamentary procedure provides an orderly, organized method for members to speak and be heard, bring important matters up before the board for consideration, and to make decisions. This is provided through the making of motions. There are four different types of motions available to the members of the board.

The first type of motion is called a main motion. In making a main motion, a member brings up an item of business for decision making. The common verbiage used is "I make a motion…" What follows can span the scope of possibilities, from procedural motions such as receiving the minutes or various reports to major purchases or policy decisions. All official decisions start with a main motion.

The second type of motion is the ability to second a motion. All main motions require a second to be considered by the board. If a main motion is made an no second is given, the motion dies and the meeting moves forward to the next point on the agenda.

The main motion and the second are the most common types of motions that will used in a church board meeting.

The third common type of motion is a privileged motion. This is used in the case of emergency issues, and addresses items not on the agenda. Major issues do come up in churches that must be addressed immediately, and this is the motion to do so. Emergency meetings and motions will be discussed in a following chapter.

The fourth and final type of motion is called an incidental motion, and it is used for procedural questions. These types of motions are focused on proper procedure, and if brought up must be considered before the other motion. These motions will most often be brought to the floor during a congregational business meeting rather than an ordinary board meeting. An example of how an incidental motion might be made could occur at a congregational meeting to call a pastor. The motion could have been made and seconded to call for an election, and during the discussion one member of the congregation might verify a quorum exists or verify proper procedure has been followed to bring the candidate before the congregation.

Incidental motions are very important to keep meetings in order and following proper procedure. These motions maintain an orderly flow of business meetings and should never be discounted or discouraged.

The presentation of motions is different in a board meeting than in a congregational setting. As this book primarily focuses upon church board meetings, I will be presenting a more informal method of presenting a motion than if one were presiding over a congregational meeting.

The items on the agenda require motions to either be received or decisions being made. Reports are given every meeting, and certain reports need to be received by the board as a matter of record. Reports that need to be received monthly are the minutes of the previous meeting and a financial report. Other reports may need to be received as well as matters of record, such as bids for large expenditures such as a bus, land or building purchase on occasion, but usually it will just be the minutes and financial report.

The other items on the agenda that may need motions are usually found in old business and new business. How to make and manage motions will be covered in the chapter on leading a board meeting. Right now, I just want to briefly follow the flow of a motion.

After a motion has been made, it must be seconded to be considered. The chair of the meeting, usually the Lead Pastor in the church setting, then asks for discussion. This is the time for members to discuss their opinion on the matter at hand, and present their arguments either for or against the issue. After all discussion has been exhausted, the chair then asks if there is any more discussion, and if there is none, calls for a vote.

Parliamentary procedure provides for an orderly voting process, eliminating the potential for most confusion. Five different voting methods are offered, and each has a situation that they work better in. Often, church by-laws will prescribe one of these methods specifically for certain types of meetings, such as the election of a pastor or board members.

The first of these five methods is the voice vote, in which those in favor of the motion vote "aye", while those opposed to the motion vote "no". This is the most common form of voting in the church board meeting. The voice vote is not counted, the louder side being the winning side. It is advisable not to use this type of vote on an issue that is closely contested or has strong opposition.

The second method is a Roll Call vote, in which each member states either "yes" or "no" as their name is called. This type of voting is more suited for a congregational meeting than a board meeting, but can also be useful in the smaller meeting.

A third type of voting is called General Consent. A general consent vote is only offered when opposition is not expected, and the chair states "If there is no objection..." and members vote their agreement by their silence. If a single member states "I object", then the matter being considered must be put to a vote by another method.

The fourth type of vote is a Vote by Division. The vote by division is similar to the voice vote in that it is not counted, unless the chair specifically requests that there is a count. Members signify their approval for the matter at hand by either standing or raising their hands, while those in opposition signify their disapproval by remaining seated or keeping their hands down, whichever the chair calls for. Like the voice vote, it is not advisable to use this type of voting on issues that might be closely contested or encounter strong opposition.

The final method of voting is the Ballot. Voting by ballot is the method to use when secrecy is important, and is often prescribed in church by-laws for votes on board members or pastor.

There are two other types of motions that can be brought up during the voting process. These motions are the Motion to Table and the Motion to Postpone Indefinitely. The motion to table simple means that members feel they need more time to consider the motion and wish to vote in a later meeting, usually the next monthly meeting. The motion to postpone is rarely used, but is a political strategy to test the strength of the resolution on the floor without taking a vote. The church board will probably use a motion to table on occasion, but probably never use a motion to postpone.

Using Parliamentary Procedure

Parliamentary procedure can be intimidating to one who is not familiar with the way it works, but it is the standard for a reason, it works very well and keeps meetings orderly and productive. Some people chafe at rules, and I understand that, for I can be that way at times also, particularly when I was younger. I have learned through experience though that adhering to parliamentary procedure faithfully in the meetings I conduct have made church business organized and efficient. It only works, like anything, if it is used properly. Here are a few guidelines to help you along the way.

First of all, don't throttle motions that you are not in favor of. Let the process play out to the finish, perhaps you might have a change of heart, I know I have had on more than one occasion as I listened to the discussion.

Second, insist on proper form. Polity might seem overbearingly formal, but it maintains order, and orderly meetings are what you want to always have. Allowing disorder or a blurring of the lines might seem harmless now, but will come back to bite you at a most inopportune time. Insist that the floor is always obtained properly. You will be grateful for your insistence upon this point when conflict and strong disagreement come. It will smooth the conflict a great deal.

Third, always speak clear and concisely, and insist others do so as well. This is particularly important when there are strong dissenting opinions on a matter of discussion. Points for and against are much stronger when spoken clearly and in a calm manner.

Finally, insist on respect at all times. People can disagree but they cannot disrespect. There is no place in a board meeting for one member to disrespect another. Every person has a unique perspective and different point of view. Scripture tell us that we don't see things clearly.

1 Cor. 13:12 WEB

For now we see in a mirror, dimly, but then face to face. Now I know in part, but then I will know fully, even as I was also fully known.

Because each member sitting around the board table see things from a dim perspective, it is only natural that there should be differences of opinion, sometimes even opposing opinions. Allow these differing opinions to be expressed, even if you do not agree with them. Simply insist on respect at all times. Board relations will be better if you do, and conflict will be resolved quicker and healthier.

Parliamentary procedure may seem intimidating and overly formal at first, but following it will make for meetings that are orderly, assist greatly in accurate record-keeping, help meetings stay on topic and flow smoothly and perhaps most importantly, make meetings a productive experience for everyone involved.

5 WRITING THE AGENDA

Have you ever been to a theatrical or community event that you couldn't wait for it to end? I know that I have on more than one occasion. At those events, I found myself very grateful for the program that had been handed out, and I would check it often, looking forward to the final act to make an appearance. The program was my lifeline, giving me hope that an end was in sight, and that I was not stuck forever. Sometimes, the agenda can function in the same manner.

The agenda is very important to the successful board meeting. The agenda gives everyone involved a clear order of business from start to finish. It keeps the meeting focused on the business at hand, allowing for all issues to be thoroughly examined to completion. Because a clear agenda will keep everyone on topic in an orderly fashion, the agenda will actually shorten the length of meetings, which all members will appreciate. In short, a well-written agenda is foundational to effective, productive board meetings.

There are a few items that need to be taken into account before actually beginning to write an agenda. The first thing to do is pray. I have found over the years in ministry that I just can't pray enough. Everything needs prayer, because everything needs God's help in one way or another. It doesn't have to be a long prayer, a detailed prayer filled with countless religious platitudes. God hears short prayers too, and He answers them. I usually pray a simple prayer when writing agendas, based off of the first of Paul's prayer in his epistle to the Ephesians.

Eph. 1:17-19 WEB

17 that the God of our Lord Jesus Christ, the Father of glory, may give to you a spirit of wisdom and revelation in the knowledge of him; 18 having the eyes of your hearts enlightened, that you may know what is the hope of his calling, and what are the riches of the glory of his inheritance in the saints, 19 and what is the exceeding

greatness of his power toward us who believe, according to that working of the strength of his might

Specifically, I pray for that "spirit of wisdom and revelation" regarding the issues that are before me, and that God would "open the eyes of (my) heart" regarding how He would have me approach each issue.

After I have prayed, I review the previous month's meeting, and review my follow-up with board members, and then begin to set the agenda for the next meeting. I will discuss follow-up and it's importance a little later in this book.

The Eight Essential Agenda Items

While there is no "one-size-fits-all" agenda that will work in every church and in every situation, I have discovered that there are eight items that every agenda needs. I have placed an example in the opposite page that you are free to copy and use as the basis of your agendas.

The eight items are the heading, opening prayer, members present, minutes, financial report, unfinished business, new business and upcoming events.

Church Board Agenda
First Amazing Church of Anywhere
Monday, August 7, 2017 6:30pm

I. **Scripture and Prayer:**

II. **Trustees Present:**

III. **Secretary's Report:**

IV. **Treasurer's Report:**

V. **Unfinished Business:**
   a.
   b.

VI. **New Business:**
   a.
   b.
   c.

VII. **Upcoming Events:**
   a.
   b.

Each of these eight items has an important purpose, and this is why I call them the essentials. I am going to briefly examine each item and explain how they work together to establish a framework for an organized, efficient and productive meeting.

The first of these items might seem unnecessary, but it serves a very important purpose. I put the name of the church, along with the time and date of the meeting. I aim to have the agenda ready and distributed to those attending a full week in advance. Putting the date and time of the meeting in the heading serves as a reminder of the meeting. The secondary purpose of this heading is for official record-keeping. While everyone already knows the name of the church they attend, for record-keeping purposes it is important that the name be there.

The second item I include on the agenda is scripture and prayer. It has, for the duration of my ministry, been my custom to begin every meeting with a brief devotional followed by prayer. By brief devotional, I mean no more than five minutes. There are a couple of reasons why I place this item first on the list of the agenda. The first reason is that I believe that we need God's leading in the business aspects of the church as much as we do during our regular services. Just as it is customary in many churches to begin Bible studies or worship services in prayer, I like to start business meeting with prayer. Besides, I truly believe that God answers prayer, and I have seen Him bring illumination and brilliant ideas to board members over the years that have blessed the churches I've served immensely. Why not ask? James told us we don't have because we don't ask, so I've decided to be one who asks all the time in every situation.

The second reason I place this item first on the agenda is a much more natural reason. People tend to run late. There is always that one person who is late to everything, no matter what. I on the other hand am an obsessively punctual person, one of those people that feels late if they are five minutes early. I also like to start on time every time (more on this later), and so placing a brief devotional at the top of the meeting does give those who are perpetually running a few minutes behind a little bit of a buffer. This allows all members to get settled and prepared to take care of church business, and serves as a reminder that we are not doing our business, but divine business.

The third item, second on the agenda, is a roll call. Because official business cannot be done without a quorum, this is extremely important to remember to confirm every meeting. A quorum is established in the church by-laws, and it is important to know how the church you serve defines it. Many churches define a quorum for church board meetings as more than fifty percent of the members present. This is also a common definition for the congregational business meeting, though some churches I have led define the congregational meeting quorum as those members in attendance. Keeping attendance, as this really is, serves more than just a legal function. It also helps establish which members are engaged in the process and which are not. An established track record of non-attendance might eventually call for an intervention by the rest of the board. Accurate attendance records are hard to argue against.

After confirming a quorum is in place, the next item on the agenda is the Secretary's report, also known as the minutes. This is the first of the business items, and I place it here because it is important to have a reminder of the previous meeting at the top of every current meeting. The minutes also serve as a legal record of the church's business transactions and decision making, so it is important that the one recording the minutes is a good note-taker.

Next on the agenda list is the financial report. Again, the location of this report is important because the board needs to be appraised of the current financial situation before making any decisions. It is also helpful to be able to immediately see any financial impact from the previous month's meeting that might have occurred. By placing the reports back to back, it is easy to see where perhaps a previous decision wasn't the best of choices, or perhaps was a stroke of genius. Either way, it is illuminating to place the two reports directly after one another.

While not on the essential items, sometimes there are other reports that need to be given. These reports are specific to multi-staff and multi-site churches, both of which I have led. I usually had the youth pastor on staff provide a report on their activities and ministry with the youth over the previous month. Once a quarter, I required our site pastor of a church we had planted in another community give a report in person to the church board. This kept the board connected and informed with the progress in both ministries. Other staff, such as our visitation pastor, I just requested a written report on activities to be presented in the meeting.

After all of the reports are presented and received by the board into the official record, it is time to address the business at hand. There are two types of business that a church will usually have, old business and new business. Old business is business that requires more than one meeting to complete, while new business is just what the title implies, new business.

Old business is placed after the reports for an orderly progression of events. Old business is, for lack of a better way of explaining it, "picking up where we left off last meeting". Not every item of business can be accomplished in one meeting. Things need follow-up, particularly when you are involved in large projects that require months of planning to complete. Examples of this include major outreach projects, hosting concerts, missions trips and the like. They also include building projects, land or building purchases, and other major purchases.

Old business is the place to ask various board members to update their status on various tasks that they have been assigned. For instance, while leading a church in Minnesota, we had a severe thunderstorm and ended up receiving severe roof damage and having our sign by the highway we were located on blown out. The re-roofing and sign repair required several months of work to complete.

First, there was the damage estimate and the insurance claim to file. Then there was the gathering of estimates, then the by-law mandated congregational meeting to approve the expenditure, followed by the selection of one bid, arrangements for the roof to be replaced, then payment. All of this took time and several meetings. The roof issue began in new business but as the process continued, it was moved to old business.

Old business also serves as an effective reminder for lower-priority tasks, and keeps little things from becoming lost and forgotten.

Immediately after old business is new business. This is the place to introduce new initiatives or decisions that need to be made. For instance, the youth pastor may want to take the youth group on a missions trip, or you want to introduce a new outreach initiative that is going to cost some money, new business is the place to introduce these ideas that need discussed and decided upon.

The final essential item on a board agenda is called upcoming events. This item serves as a reminder of events that the church has planned over the upcoming month. Any number of events can be placed in this item, from a senior's trip to a gospel concert to the youth group's bowling night to a couple's retreat the third weekend of the month. It is a helpful item to keep essential items before the board to keep communication clear.

These eight items on your agenda will keep your meetings orderly, accomplishing tasks efficiently and assist greatly in official record-keeping.

6 CALLING A BOARD MEETING

Calling a board meeting is the next step in conducting a board meeting. I strongly suggest establishing a recurring schedule for board meetings, so that both you and your board members can pre-plan for the meeting on a monthly basis. I use the second Monday of every month. This way, the board knows that on the first Monday of each month, I will email them a copy of the agenda. If they have items that they wish to see on the agenda, they know that they need to contact me before that date. Regularly scheduled meetings bring order to the meeting process that can easily spiral out of control.

Regularly scheduled meetings also establish pre-arranged due dates for reports, research that may need to be done between meetings, and task accomplishment. In this sense, they help members be prepared for the meetings, and prepared members always results in more productive meetings. Regularly scheduled meetings also increases regular attendance of meetings, which again smooths the entire process greatly. People tend to remember a regularly occurring event better than irregularly occurring events. There is nothing worse than looking at one or two board members who have given of their time to attend this meeting, and having to send them home, essentially wasting their evening that they could have spent with their families because a quorum was not attained.

As I mentioned above, it is my habit to submit the upcoming meeting's agenda to those who will attend one week prior to the meeting. I do this for several reasons.

The first reason I think it is important to present the agenda early is that it acts as a reminder that there is a meeting coming up soon. This helps reduce the "I forgot" excuse. It also helps members remember to clear their schedule for the meeting, so there will not be any conflicts that could have been avoided.

Having a regularly scheduled board meeting also board members a week to get the research they were assigned done prior to the meeting or complete any tasks that they were assigned in the previous meeting. While the church is usually the first priority in the life of a minister, it usually falls below family, job and leisure activities in the lives of most attendees. Personally, I see nothing wrong with this. Because of the tendency for church responsibilities to be a little lower priority, it is helpful to have that little extra friendly reminder to get this or that done before the meeting.

Sometimes, there are issues on the table that really need some serious consideration and soul-searching to come to a decision on. It may a positive but major decision such as deciding to re-locate the church or make a major purchase or pursue a radically different approach to gospel work in the community. It may be a matter of grave concern or doctrinal point spanning from church discipline to leaving the denomination. Serious issues come up and sometimes it is really nice for members to receive that little reminder in their email box that they need to take the time to consider the matter at hand. I have several times over the years been thanked by board members for providing the agenda early for them. This is a little action that goes a long way, and lets then know that you are considering them in the grand scheme of things.

Board members that feel considered are easier to work with.

7 THE BOARD MEETING

On the night of the meeting, I make an effort to be at the church at least one hour before the meeting is scheduled to begin to make sure everything is in order. Arriving early is an important part of setting the tone for a positive, productive and successful meeting. There is no worse way to start a meeting than rushing in at the last minute frazzled and unprepared.

Arriving early allows you to prepare any refreshments that might be offered. I suggest preparing coffee, de-caf, hot water for tea and cold water, depending upon what the members prefer. While the coffee is brewing and the water heating, take a moment to review the agenda one more time. It is good to be certain of each item up for discussion. It is also good to make a few extra copies of the agenda and any other reports and paperwork that you have received, in case a member or two forgets to bring theirs.

After all of the pre-meeting preparation is completed, take some time to pray and wait upon the Lord. He is your strength in ministry, and whether or not you will be discussing some hard issues at the meeting, it is good to spend some time settling your own soul so that you are not only prepared materially and organizationally but also spiritually.

As the scheduled time for the meeting draws near and members begin to arrive, greet each one in a friendly and confident manner. Verify that they have all of the necessary paperwork and if not, give them some of the extras that you have prepared. Guide them to the room prepared for the meeting as soon as possible. You want to respect member's time begin the meeting as soon as a quorum is reached.

The Meeting

As soon as the necessary number of members has arrived to form the quorum, it is time for the meeting to begin. Avoid the temptation to fellowship and talk about the local football team or events that have happened in the community, it is time to accomplish the task at hand. This is a big part of respecting member's time, and respecting their time will gain you great favor over the years. From this time until the conclusion of the meeting, follow the agenda as closely as possible. The only exception to this is in the event of an emergency, which I will discuss later.

Keep the conversation throughout the course of the meeting on the agenda item currently up for discussion. This can be a tricky task some times as conversation can easily go from one point to another at the speed of light. I have often had board members begin discussion on one item on the agenda only to jump to another that perhaps they have some real interest in or something to report about. This will happen on a regular basis, so be prepared to kindly, respectfully yet firmly remind them of the topic at hand, such as "We will discuss that in just a moment, we have to finish receiving the financial report first." Simple reminders like that bring them back to the business at hand and help move them along to what they really want to talk about anyway. Board members appreciate the chair keeping meetings in order.

Members stay engaged in the meeting as the chair keeps to the agenda, and productivity increases as a result of quickly bringing the meeting back into line. Many church leaders do not appreciate the power of productivity in board meetings, thinking of that in terms of secular work or the corporate world, but church board meetings can be highly productive if simple procedures are followed such as sticking to the agenda.

I have again placed the sample agenda posted previously to aid in the discussion here.

Church Board Agenda
First Amazing Church of Anywhere
Monday, August 7, 2017 6:30pm

I. Scripture and Prayer:

II. Trustees Present:

III. Secretary's Report:

IV. Treasurer's Report:

V. Unfinished Business:
   a.
   b.

VI. New Business:
   a.
   b.
   c.

VII. Upcoming Events:
   a.
   b.

Move smoothly from point to point. As the meeting opens, begin with a simple prayer. God hears short prayers as well as long one, and doesn't pay more attention to long ones. Ask God to help with the meeting and to bring revelation, good ideas and direction. Move to a brief devotional, and by brief, I mean no more than five minutes. It is here that I take attendance, noting those who are present to verify a legal quorum. After concluding the devotional and attendance, move immediately to the minutes. My practice has been to email the minutes along with the agenda one week early so that members can read it in advance, so the need is only to ask if there are any questions or corrections observed and if not, as for a motion to receive.

As soon as the motion to receive is completed, I move immediately to the financial report. Again, the report should have been included in the email with the agenda and minutes, so members have had a week to look over the financials. This allows the Treasurer to focus on the important aspects of their report such as major expenditures, month-end profit or loss and important year-to-date line items.

After the report, I ask if there are any questions, then ask for a motion to receive as presented or amended. After the financial report is received, I ask for any other reports that might need to be given, and if there are none, I move on to old business.

As I stated before, it is very important for there to be no more than five, six at the very most, items of business between old and new business. This is where meetings can get bogged down quickly.

The old business is to remind members of projects started that are still incomplete or in process. One example of old business happened while I was leading a church in Minnesota. I came back from my Christmas/New Year vacation on a Sunday morning to discover the sanctuary was 55 degrees, and it was about -20F outside. I investigated the five furnaces we had and found two of them were out of commission. This began a process of replacing all five furnaces and took a few meetings to accomplish. Most of the times the furnaces appeared on the agenda, they were in old business. We had them fixed temporarily, but they had exceeded their lifespan and needed replaced.

The old business then consisted of receipt of bids, and the two members assigned to collect bids reported them, at which time we voted to receive one bid. Then one member was assigned to make the arrangements for the purchase of the furnaces and their installation. Some of the information was transmitted to me between meetings, and full information was given at the next meeting, again under old business. A final report was given under the old business line in a subsequent meeting, the process completed.

This is how old business works, use it to keep job moving along and information flowing.

After the items under old business are completed, move to new business. New business items should only appear once and then move to old business if they need to be addressed in additional meetings. It is best if most business occurs under old business, with new business added as old business tasks are completed. There are usually a few one-time items that do need addressed under new business, such as funding requests and scheduling items.

After discussing and voting on the new business items, don't succumb to the temptation to take multiple new items, unless they are of an emergency nature. Doing so will breed a chaos into your meetings that will rob productivity and time management. Move to any upcoming events that the board members will need to be aware of, major events, a church picnic, graduation and events of this nature.

After this brief reminder, it is time to close the meeting. Close with a word of prayer and dismiss. Members are usually happy to go, and a well-organized, agenda-driven meeting keeps the mood positive and with a sense of production throughout the meeting. Smiles on members faces as they depart is a sign of a good meeting.

Usually after the dismissal, one or two members might stick around to talk. Sometimes they want to talk about items discussed in the meeting "off the record". When they attempt to do so, politely but firmly say something to the effect of "that needs to be taken up with the whole board." This usually will draw agreement, but sometimes they will persist. Do not give into this pressure, for it will sow chaos and power struggles into your board meetings that only serve as distractions and create division where unity in Christ should reign. If they are insistent, remind them that your policy is only to discuss board matters with the entire board, and you simply cannot make exceptions.

On the other hand, some members might just want to small talk a little, make sure you engage them in that. Sports teams, local events, their relationship with God, these are all great topics. Even if you're not a sports fan, it helps to connect with your people if you know basic information such as standings and scores, maybe the team superstar. Small talk builds relationships that go a long way down the road, don't shy away from it. It builds morale and comradery.

Don't let the chatter go on too long after the meeting, as you know that they want to get home and so do you. After about 15 minutes, I advise getting up and begin turning things off, kindly letting them know you've got to be leaving soon.

Remember, make respecting their time a priority, and you will find your meetings go quickly and get a lot accomplished. This is how successful meetings work, quickly, efficiently and productively.

8 AFTER THE MEETING

The conclusion of a good meeting is a good feeling. Because board meetings are an unavoidable fact of a pastor's life, I prefer them to be good meetings. I enjoy locking the church doors and heading to my car, knowing that we had a productive meeting and it is not too late. I feel energized in moments like this. The conclusion of a meeting is not the conclusion of business however.

This chapter address steps to take after the meeting has concluded, to set the stage for productive meeting after productive meeting. As I wrote about before specifically addressing the meeting itself, there is a lot of preparation that goes into a successful meeting. My advice is to get right to work on the results of the meeting to perpetuate the good feelings and teamwork that were exhibited the night before.

If at all possible, set aside time the day after the meeting, preferably in the morning to review the previous night's meeting. Examine what went well, what could have gone better and what didn't go well at all. Don't shy away from the bad moments, they do come up. Not everyone sees eye to eye at all times. As you consider the meeting, consider what was said that was positive, and what was negative. Consider ways you could react better if you feel you reacted out of sorts, and consider ways you might be able to reach a board member who might be upset and currently seem both unreasonable and unreachable.

After you have spent some time examining the meeting, turn your attention to any tasks that might have been assigned the night before. Record who was assigned which task, for this will go under unfinished business on the next agenda. After confirming which tasks were assigned to the various board members, turn to the tasks that were assigned to you.

This is a very important part of a successful board meeting. You, as pastor, set the example for the completion of tasks among all of your leadership team. If you are slothful and undependable, your example will be followed by members of the board. If you are late to complete tasks, members will assume it is fine if they are late to complete as well. I can tell you from experience it is not a pleasant feeling to have tasks that needed completion forgotten or put off, and your hands are tied until they are completed. Meetings that are short but unfulfilled do not leave one with a good feeling at their conclusion.

Organize the tasks assigned to you and plot out a course of action to accomplish them in a timely manner. If needed, create reminders for yourself to keep yourself on track.

Create a schedule over the course of the next month to follow up with board members about the tasks assigned to them. A friendly phone call with two weeks to go until the next meeting can remind them to get the job done without feeling nagged and pressured.

Be obsessive about keeping records. This helps you build an agenda that will guide your next meeting through to success. Know who is to accomplish what, where you need to check up and what you are to do. Keep documentation of all that you do, so that you can set an example of complete work. Documentation is important, and setting the example will help board members do the same and prevent awkward moments during meetings.

Finally, two weeks out from the next meeting, begin preparing the agenda, using your documentation from the previous meeting and any information you have received in the time since the last meeting. Always stay ahead in this area to keep your meetings organized, productive and successful.

9 EMERGENCY MEETINGS

The final issue I will address in this book is the emergency meeting. Unfortunately, we live in an age of moral ambiguity. We also live in an age of litigation. Because of this, sometimes an emergency situation comes up that must be addressed.

The evening news has been filled with too many stories of sexual misconduct in churches, with both pastor and parishioner being accused. Any accusation of any form of sexual misconduct must be addressed immediately.

Other forms of misconduct can also occur in the church, such as embezzlement, physical or emotional abuse, abuse of position, the list seems endless.

All of these forms of misconduct can, and often do, lead to a lawsuit. Misconduct is not the only way a church can have an emergency. A serious injury, such as someone slipping on an icy sidewalk or some other mishap can also create an emergency that must be immediately addressed.

Finally, weather or building failure of some form can also create an emergency, such as the failure of the church furnaces in a Minnesota winter I experienced. We also had a roof damaged heavily by high winds or a small tornado at that church, and where I am now in the Caribbean we were hit by the eye of Hurricane Maria at its greatest intensity, with 175mph sustained winds and gusts far beyond. We lost three buildings and incurred major damage all around. These also require emergency meetings.

The first rule of an emergency meeting is to call it for as soon as possible, with the second being that it is exclusively for the conduction of business directly related to the emergency at hand. In all three of these instances, there may be a need for filing an insurance claim. Make sure that you have a copy of the policy in full before the beginning of the meeting.

The next page gives a sample agenda for an emergency meeting.

Church Board Agenda
First Amazing Church of Anywhere
Emergency Meeting
Monday, August 7, 2017 6:30pm

I. **Scripture and Prayer:**

II. **Trustees Present:**

III. **The Issue at Hand:**

IV. **Insurance Policy:**

The agenda needs to be short and very direct. Open in prayer for guidance, give a short devotional perhaps demonstrating that God has given guidance to those that ask from scripture. Take attendance to officially confirm a quorum and then move immediately to business.

Address the reason for meeting in a matter of fact tone of voice, no matter the gravity of the situation. If there is the accusation of misconduct of any kind, don't downplay the accusation, bring it out in the open and deal with it. Allow each member to speak their mind on the matter, don't say to much until everyone else has spoken.

If it is an injury and potential lawsuit, follow the same course of action, let each one speak, don't say much or anything at all until the others have spoken and then summarize what they said.

In the matter of a building issue, let others share their sense of loss before you do. When we lost our thrift shop, a new building not fully constructed and our sanctuary, the roof sustaining two massive holes in the roof and the sanctuary completely destroyed, I simply said "Wow." What else was there to say, we were completely totaled as a church. They each needed the opportunity to try to come to grips with the magnitude of destruction we had experienced.

No matter what the issue is, address it straight forward, don't downplay anything, and allow your board to talk. After they have said their piece and feel like they have put their feelings and perspectives on the table, then move to the business of the matter.

First of all, craft a response. The response can include an investigation of the accusation of misconduct, investigation of the conditions at the time of the injury, or property damage. After crafting a response, turn to the insurance policy.

For sexual abuse and other forms of misconduct, as well as any injury and liability claims, look to your policy for coverage in those sections and contact your insurance agent.

For building damage, contact your agent and schedule an appointment to get an adjuster to your property to begin the claim process. It is advisable to take as much photo and video documentation as you can and if possible, leave the damage alone until after the claims adjuster has made an initial visit.

Finally, most emergency meetings will require follow-up, and it is best to handle them separate at first until the process has moved further along and you know what you're dealing with. If you can keep regular church business separate from the emergency for two or three meetings, you will find your people more productive and the times you gather to address the emergency issue will result in better planning and address of the emergency.

May God's blessing be on you as you serve His Kingdom and His people in Jesus name.

Pastor Jeff continues to serve the people of the Caribbean at the time of this writing and prays that this guide will be helpful to all who are just setting out into the world of ministry.

www.ingramcontent.com/pod-product-compliance
Lightning Source LLC
Chambersburg PA
CBHW031928240526
45464CB00023B/2567